Monthly Organizer

BELONGS TO:

_____

_____

_____

A SPECIAL REQUEST

"If you enjoy this book , could you please do me a favor ?

Please take a moment to leave your review on Amazon review page for our books.

Please spare your time to write just a few words , it would help us a lot!

Thank you for your support!

JOHAN PUBLISHERS

Website :   JohanPublishers.com

Email :   johanpublishers1@gmail.com

Facebook :   www.facebook.com/Johanpublisher

Pinterest :   www.pinterest.com/johanpublishers

PERSONAL CONTACT

Name : ....

Address : ....

....

Phone : ....

E-Mail : ....

BUSINESS CONTACT

Name : ....

Address : ....

....

Phone : ....

E-Mail : ....

EMERGENCY CONTACT

Name : ....

Phone : ....

E-Mail : ....

Doctor's Name : ....

Phone : ....

E-Mail : ....

Police : ....

Phone : ....

E-Mail : ....

Name : ....

Phone : ....

E-Mail : ....

Name : ....

Phone : ....

E-Mail : ....

Fire : ....

Phone : ....

E-Mail : ....

MEMO

_____ _____
_____ _____
_____ _____
_____ _____
_____ _____

LIST OF INCOME

MONTH		YEAR	

No.	SOURCE OF INCOME	AMOUNT	DATE
TOTAL INCOME			

SAVING AND INVESTMENT

No.	SAVING AND INVESTMENT	AMOUNT	DATE
TOTAL			

NOTE

Monthly Expenses

Car

	$
	$
	$
	$
	$

Food

	$
	$
	$
	$
	$

Housing

	$
	$
	$
	$
	$

School and Work

	$
	$
	$
	$
	$

Pets

	$
	$
	$
	$
	$

Utilities

	$
	$
	$
	$
	$

Personal Expenses

	$
	$
	$
	$
	$

Donation/Charity

	$
	$
	$
	$
	$

Health

	$
	$
	$
	$
	$

Kids Expenses

	$
	$
	$
	$
	$

Travel

	$
	$
	$
	$
	$

Miscellaneous Expenses

	$
	$
	$
	$
	$

Notes

BILL TRACKER   MONTH : ....

Payable To	Amount	Due Date	Paid
			☐
			☐
			☐
			☐
			☐
			☐
			☐
			☐
			☐
			☐
			☐
			☐
			☐
			☐
			☐
			☐
			☐
			☐
			☐
TOTAL PAYABLES			

BILL TRACKER   MONTH : ....

Payable To	Amount	Due Date	Paid
			☐
			☐
			☐
			☐
			☐
			☐
			☐
			☐
			☐
			☐
			☐
			☐
			☐
			☐
			☐
			☐
			☐
			☐
			☐
TOTAL PAYABLES			

WEEKLY EXPENSES TRACKER

MONTH		BUDGET	

MONDAY

Description	Amount

TUESDAY

Description	Amount

WEDNESDAY

Description	Amount

THURSDAY

Description	Amount

WEEKLY EXPENSE TRACKER

TOTAL EXPENSES			BALANCE	

FRIDAY

Description	Amount

SATURDAY

Description	Amount

SUNDAY

Description	Amount

NOTES

WEEKLY EXPENSES TRACKER

MONTH		BUDGET	

MONDAY

Description	Amount

TUESDAY

Description	Amount

WEDNESDAY

Description	Amount

THURSDAY

Description	Amount

WEEKLY EXPENSE TRACKER

TOTAL EXPENSES	

BALANCE	

FRIDAY

Description	Amount

SATURDAY

Description	Amount

SUNDAY

Description	Amount

NOTES

WEEKLY EXPENSES TRACKER

MONTH		BUDGET	

MONDAY

Description	Amount

TUESDAY

Description	Amount

WEDNESDAY

Description	Amount

THURSDAY

Description	Amount

WEEKLY EXPENSE TRACKER

TOTAL EXPENSES		BALANCE	

FRIDAY

Description	Amount

SATURDAY

Description	Amount

SUNDAY

Description	Amount

NOTES

WEEKLY EXPENSES TRACKER

MONTH		BUDGET	

MONDAY

Description	Amount

TUESDAY

Description	Amount

WEDNESDAY

Description	Amount

THURSDAY

Description	Amount

WEEKLY EXPENSE TRACKER

TOTAL EXPENSES		BALANCE	

FRIDAY

Description	Amount

SATURDAY

Description	Amount

SUNDAY

Description	Amount

NOTES

WEEKLY EXPENSES TRACKER

MONTH		BUDGET	

MONDAY

Description	Amount

TUESDAY

Description	Amount

WEDNESDAY

Description	Amount

THURSDAY

Description	Amount

WEEKLY EXPENSE TRACKER

TOTAL EXPENSES		BALANCE	

FRIDAY

Description	Amount

SATURDAY

Description	Amount

SUNDAY

Description	Amount

NOTES

NOTE

NOTE

LIST OF INCOME

MONTH		YEAR	

No.	SOURCE OF INCOME	AMOUNT	DATE
TOTAL INCOME			

SAVING AND INVESTMENT

No.	SAVING AND INVESTMENT	AMOUNT	DATE
TOTAL			

NOTE

Monthly Expenses

MONTH

YEAR

Car

	$
	$
	$
	$
	$

Food

	$
	$
	$
	$
	$

Housing

	$
	$
	$
	$
	$

School and Work

	$
	$
	$
	$
	$

Pets

	$
	$
	$
	$
	$

Utilities

	$
	$
	$
	$
	$

Personal Expenses

	$
	$
	$
	$
	$

Donation/Charity

	$
	$
	$
	$
	$

Health

	$
	$
	$
	$
	$

Kids Expenses

	$
	$
	$
	$
	$

Travel

	$
	$
	$
	$
	$

Miscellaneous Expenses

	$
	$
	$
	$
	$

Notes

BILL TRACKER

MONTH : ....

Payable To	Amount	Due Date	Paid
			☐
			☐
			☐
			☐
			☐
			☐
			☐
			☐
			☐
			☐
			☐
			☐
			☐
			☐
			☐
			☐
			☐
			☐
TOTAL PAYABLES			

BILL TRACKER

MONTH : . . . .

Payable To	Amount	Due Date	Paid
			☐
			☐
			☐
			☐
			☐
			☐
			☐
			☐
			☐
			☐
			☐
			☐
			☐
			☐
			☐
			☐
			☐
			☐
TOTAL PAYABLES			

WEEKLY EXPENSES TRACKER

MONTH		BUDGET	

MONDAY

Description	Amount

TUESDAY

Description	Amount

WEDNESDAY

Description	Amount

THURSDAY

Description	Amount

WEEKLY EXPENSE TRACKER

TOTAL EXPENSES	

BALANCE	

FRIDAY

Description	Amount

SATURDAY

Description	Amount

SUNDAY

Description	Amount

NOTES

WEEKLY EXPENSES TRACKER

MONTH		BUDGET	

MONDAY

Description	Amount

TUESDAY

Description	Amount

WEDNESDAY

Description	Amount

THURSDAY

Description	Amount

WEEKLY EXPENSE TRACKER

TOTAL EXPENSES		BALANCE	

FRIDAY

Description	Amount

SATURDAY

Description	Amount

SUNDAY

Description	Amount

NOTES

WEEKLY EXPENSES TRACKER

MONTH	

BUDGET	

MONDAY

Description	Amount

TUESDAY

Description	Amount

WEDNESDAY

Description	Amount

THURSDAY

Description	Amount

WEEKLY EXPENSE TRACKER

TOTAL EXPENSES		BALANCE	

FRIDAY

Description	Amount

SATURDAY

Description	Amount

SUNDAY

Description	Amount

NOTES

WEEKLY EXPENSES TRACKER

MONTH		BUDGET	

MONDAY

Description	Amount

TUESDAY

Description	Amount

WEDNESDAY

Description	Amount

THURSDAY

Description	Amount

WEEKLY EXPENSE TRACKER

TOTAL EXPENSES		BALANCE	

FRIDAY

Description	Amount

SATURDAY

Description	Amount

SUNDAY

Description	Amount

NOTES

WEEKLY EXPENSES TRACKER

MONTH	

BUDGET	

MONDAY

Description	Amount

TUESDAY

Description	Amount

WEDNESDAY

Description	Amount

THURSDAY

Description	Amount

WEEKLY EXPENSE TRACKER

TOTAL EXPENSES		BALANCE	

FRIDAY

Description	Amount

SATURDAY

Description	Amount

SUNDAY

Description	Amount

NOTES

NOTE

NOTE

LIST OF INCOME

MONTH		YEAR	

No.	SOURCE OF INCOME	AMOUNT	DATE
TOTAL INCOME			

SAVING AND INVESTMENT

No.	SAVING AND INVESTMENT	AMOUNT	DATE
TOTAL			

NOTE

Monthly Expenses

Car

	$
	$
	$
	$
	$

Food

	$
	$
	$
	$
	$

Housing

	$
	$
	$
	$
	$

School and Work

	$
	$
	$
	$
	$

Pets

	$
	$
	$
	$
	$

Utilities

	$
	$
	$
	$
	$

Personal Expenses

	$
	$
	$
	$
	$

Donation/Charity

	$
	$
	$
	$
	$

Health

	$
	$
	$
	$
	$

Kids Expenses

	$
	$
	$
	$
	$

Travel

	$
	$
	$
	$
	$

Miscellaneous Expenses

	$
	$
	$
	$
	$

Notes

BILL TRACKER MONTH : ....

Payable To	Amount	Due Date	Paid
			☐
			☐
			☐
			☐
			☐
			☐
			☐
			☐
			☐
			☐
			☐
			☐
			☐
			☐
			☐
			☐
			☐
			☐
			☐
TOTAL PAYABLES			

BILL TRACKER

MONTH : ....

Payable To	Amount	Due Date	Paid
			☐
			☐
			☐
			☐
			☐
			☐
			☐
			☐
			☐
			☐
			☐
			☐
			☐
			☐
			☐
			☐
			☐
			☐
TOTAL PAYABLES			

WEEKLY EXPENSES TRACKER

MONTH		BUDGET	

MONDAY

Description	Amount

TUESDAY

Description	Amount

WEDNESDAY

Description	Amount

THURSDAY

Description	Amount

WEEKLY EXPENSE TRACKER

TOTAL EXPENSES	

BALANCE	

FRIDAY

Description	Amount

SATURDAY

Description	Amount

SUNDAY

Description	Amount

NOTES

WEEKLY EXPENSES TRACKER

MONTH		BUDGET	

MONDAY

Description	Amount

TUESDAY

Description	Amount

WEDNESDAY

Description	Amount

THURSDAY

Description	Amount

WEEKLY EXPENSE TRACKER

TOTAL EXPENSES		BALANCE	

FRIDAY

Description	Amount

SATURDAY

Description	Amount

SUNDAY

Description	Amount

NOTES

WEEKLY EXPENSES TRACKER

MONTH		BUDGET	

MONDAY

Description	Amount

TUESDAY

Description	Amount

WEDNESDAY

Description	Amount

THURSDAY

Description	Amount

WEEKLY EXPENSE TRACKER

TOTAL EXPENSES		BALANCE	

FRIDAY

Description	Amount

SATURDAY

Description	Amount

SUNDAY

Description	Amount

NOTES

WEEKLY EXPENSES TRACKER

MONTH		BUDGET	

MONDAY

Description	Amount

TUESDAY

Description	Amount

WEDNESDAY

Description	Amount

THURSDAY

Description	Amount

WEEKLY EXPENSE TRACKER

TOTAL EXPENSES		BALANCE	

FRIDAY

Description	Amount

SATURDAY

Description	Amount

SUNDAY

Description	Amount

NOTES

WEEKLY EXPENSES TRACKER

MONTH		BUDGET	

MONDAY

Description	Amount

TUESDAY

Description	Amount

WEDNESDAY

Description	Amount

THURSDAY

Description	Amount

WEEKLY EXPENSE TRACKER

TOTAL EXPENSES		BALANCE	

FRIDAY

Description	Amount

SATURDAY

Description	Amount

SUNDAY

Description	Amount

NOTES

NOTE

NOTE

LIST OF INCOME

MONTH		YEAR	

No.	SOURCE OF INCOME	AMOUNT	DATE
TOTAL INCOME			

SAVING AND INVESTMENT

No.	SAVING AND INVESTMENT	AMOUNT	DATE
TOTAL			

NOTE

Monthly Expenses

Car

	$
	$
	$
	$
	$

Food

	$
	$
	$
	$
	$

Housing

	$
	$
	$
	$
	$

School and Work

	$
	$
	$
	$
	$

Pets

	$
	$
	$
	$
	$

Utilities

	$
	$
	$
	$
	$

Personal Expenses

	$
	$
	$
	$
	$

Donation/Charity

	$
	$
	$
	$
	$

Health

	$
	$
	$
	$
	$

Kids Expenses

	$
	$
	$
	$
	$

Travel

	$
	$
	$
	$
	$

Miscellaneous Expenses

	$
	$
	$
	$
	$

Notes

BILL TRACKER

MONTH : ....

Payable To	Amount	Due Date	Paid
			☐
			☐
			☐
			☐
			☐
			☐
			☐
			☐
			☐
			☐
			☐
			☐
			☐
			☐
			☐
			☐
			☐
			☐
TOTAL PAYABLES			

BILL TRACKER   MONTH : ....

Payable To	Amount	Due Date	Paid
			☐
			☐
			☐
			☐
			☐
			☐
			☐
			☐
			☐
			☐
			☐
			☐
			☐
			☐
			☐
			☐
			☐
			☐
TOTAL PAYABLES			

WEEKLY EXPENSES TRACKER

MONTH		BUDGET	

MONDAY

Description	Amount

TUESDAY

Description	Amount

WEDNESDAY

Description	Amount

THURSDAY

Description	Amount

WEEKLY EXPENSE TRACKER

TOTAL EXPENSES		BALANCE	

FRIDAY

Description	Amount

SATURDAY

Description	Amount

SUNDAY

Description	Amount

NOTES

WEEKLY EXPENSES TRACKER

MONTH	

BUDGET	

MONDAY

Description	Amount

TUESDAY

Description	Amount

WEDNESDAY

Description	Amount

THURSDAY

Description	Amount

WEEKLY EXPENSE TRACKER

TOTAL EXPENSES		BALANCE	

FRIDAY

Description	Amount

SATURDAY

Description	Amount

SUNDAY

Description	Amount

NOTES

WEEKLY EXPENSES TRACKER

MONTH	

BUDGET	

MONDAY

Description	Amount

TUESDAY

Description	Amount

WEDNESDAY

Description	Amount

THURSDAY

Description	Amount

WEEKLY EXPENSE TRACKER

TOTAL EXPENSES	

BALANCE	

FRIDAY

Description	Amount

SATURDAY

Description	Amount

SUNDAY

Description	Amount

NOTES

WEEKLY EXPENSES TRACKER

MONTH		BUDGET	

MONDAY

Description	Amount

TUESDAY

Description	Amount

WEDNESDAY

Description	Amount

THURSDAY

Description	Amount

WEEKLY EXPENSE TRACKER

TOTAL EXPENSES		BALANCE	

FRIDAY

Description	Amount

SATURDAY

Description	Amount

SUNDAY

Description	Amount

NOTES

WEEKLY EXPENSES TRACKER

MONTH		BUDGET	

MONDAY

Description	Amount

TUESDAY

Description	Amount

WEDNESDAY

Description	Amount

THURSDAY

Description	Amount

WEEKLY EXPENSE TRACKER

TOTAL EXPENSES		BALANCE	

FRIDAY

Description	Amount

SATURDAY

Description	Amount

SUNDAY

Description	Amount

NOTES

NOTE

NOTE

LIST OF INCOME

MONTH		YEAR	

No.	SOURCE OF INCOME	AMOUNT	DATE
TOTAL INCOME			

SAVING AND INVESTMENT

No.	SAVING AND INVESTMENT	AMOUNT	DATE
TOTAL			

NOTE

Monthly Expenses

MONTH [_____]   **YEAR** [_____]

Car

	$
	$
	$
	$
	$

Food

	$
	$
	$
	$
	$

Housing

	$
	$
	$
	$
	$

School and Work

	$
	$
	$
	$
	$

Pets

	$
	$
	$
	$
	$

Utilities

	$
	$
	$
	$
	$

Personal Expenses

	$
	$
	$
	$
	$

Donation/Charity

	$
	$
	$
	$
	$

Health

	$
	$
	$
	$
	$

Kids Expenses

	$
	$
	$
	$
	$

Travel

	$
	$
	$
	$
	$

Miscellaneous Expenses

	$
	$
	$
	$
	$

Notes

BILL TRACKER

MONTH : ....

Payable To	Amount	Due Date	Paid
			☐
			☐
			☐
			☐
			☐
			☐
			☐
			☐
			☐
			☐
			☐
			☐
			☐
			☐
			☐
			☐
			☐
			☐
TOTAL PAYABLES			

BILL TRACKER

MONTH : ....

Payable To	Amount	Due Date	Paid
			☐
			☐
			☐
			☐
			☐
			☐
			☐
			☐
			☐
			☐
			☐
			☐
			☐
			☐
			☐
			☐
			☐
			☐
			☐
TOTAL PAYABLES			

WEEKLY EXPENSES TRACKER

MONTH		BUDGET	

MONDAY

Description	Amount

TUESDAY

Description	Amount

WEDNESDAY

Description	Amount

THURSDAY

Description	Amount

WEEKLY EXPENSE TRACKER

TOTAL EXPENSES		BALANCE	

FRIDAY

Description	Amount

SATURDAY

Description	Amount

SUNDAY

Description	Amount

NOTES

WEEKLY EXPENSES TRACKER

MONTH		BUDGET	

MONDAY

Description	Amount

TUESDAY

Description	Amount

WEDNESDAY

Description	Amount

THURSDAY

Description	Amount

WEEKLY EXPENSE TRACKER

TOTAL EXPENSES		BALANCE	

FRIDAY

Description	Amount

SATURDAY

Description	Amount

SUNDAY

Description	Amount

NOTES

WEEKLY EXPENSES TRACKER

MONTH		BUDGET	

MONDAY

Description	Amount

TUESDAY

Description	Amount

WEDNESDAY

Description	Amount

THURSDAY

Description	Amount

WEEKLY EXPENSE TRACKER

TOTAL EXPENSES	

BALANCE	

FRIDAY

Description	Amount

SATURDAY

Description	Amount

SUNDAY

Description	Amount

NOTES

WEEKLY EXPENSES TRACKER

MONTH		BUDGET	

MONDAY

Description	Amount

TUESDAY

Description	Amount

WEDNESDAY

Description	Amount

THURSDAY

Description	Amount

WEEKLY EXPENSE TRACKER

TOTAL EXPENSES		BALANCE	

FRIDAY

Description	Amount

SATURDAY

Description	Amount

SUNDAY

Description	Amount

NOTES

WEEKLY EXPENSES TRACKER

MONTH		BUDGET	

MONDAY

Description	Amount

TUESDAY

Description	Amount

WEDNESDAY

Description	Amount

THURSDAY

Description	Amount

WEEKLY EXPENSE TRACKER

TOTAL EXPENSES		BALANCE	

FRIDAY

Description	Amount

SATURDAY

Description	Amount

SUNDAY

Description	Amount

NOTES

NOTE

NOTE

LIST OF INCOME

MONTH		YEAR	

No.	SOURCE OF INCOME	AMOUNT	DATE
TOTAL INCOME			

SAVING AND INVESTMENT

No.	SAVING AND INVESTMENT	AMOUNT	DATE
TOTAL			

NOTE

Monthly Expenses

MONTH _____   **YEAR** _____

Car

	$
	$
	$
	$
	$

Food

	$
	$
	$
	$
	$

Housing

	$
	$
	$
	$
	$

School and Work

	$
	$
	$
	$
	$

Pets

	$
	$
	$
	$
	$

Utilities

	$
	$
	$
	$
	$

Personal Expenses

	$
	$
	$
	$
	$

Donation/Charity

	$
	$
	$
	$
	$

Health

	$
	$
	$
	$
	$

Kids Expenses

	$
	$
	$
	$
	$

Travel

	$
	$
	$
	$
	$

Miscellaneous Expenses

	$
	$
	$
	$
	$

Notes

BILL TRACKER

MONTH : ....

Payable To	Amount	Due Date	Paid
			☐
			☐
			☐
			☐
			☐
			☐
			☐
			☐
			☐
			☐
			☐
			☐
			☐
			☐
			☐
			☐
			☐
			☐
TOTAL PAYABLES			

BILL TRACKER

MONTH : ....

Payable To	Amount	Due Date	Paid
			☐
			☐
			☐
			☐
			☐
			☐
			☐
			☐
			☐
			☐
			☐
			☐
			☐
			☐
			☐
			☐
			☐
			☐
			☐
TOTAL PAYABLES			

WEEKLY EXPENSES TRACKER

MONTH		BUDGET	

MONDAY

Description	Amount

TUESDAY

Description	Amount

WEDNESDAY

Description	Amount

THURSDAY

Description	Amount

WEEKLY EXPENSE TRACKER

TOTAL EXPENSES		BALANCE	

FRIDAY

Description	Amount

SATURDAY

Description	Amount

SUNDAY

Description	Amount

NOTES

WEEKLY EXPENSES TRACKER

MONTH		BUDGET	

MONDAY

Description	Amount

TUESDAY

Description	Amount

WEDNESDAY

Description	Amount

THURSDAY

Description	Amount

WEEKLY EXPENSE TRACKER

TOTAL EXPENSES			BALANCE	

FRIDAY

Description	Amount

SATURDAY

Description	Amount

SUNDAY

Description	Amount

NOTES

WEEKLY EXPENSES TRACKER

MONTH		BUDGET	

MONDAY

Description	Amount

TUESDAY

Description	Amount

WEDNESDAY

Description	Amount

THURSDAY

Description	Amount

WEEKLY EXPENSE TRACKER

TOTAL EXPENSES		BALANCE	

FRIDAY

Description	Amount

SATURDAY

Description	Amount

SUNDAY

Description	Amount

NOTES

WEEKLY EXPENSES TRACKER

MONTH		BUDGET	

MONDAY

Description	Amount

TUESDAY

Description	Amount

WEDNESDAY

Description	Amount

THURSDAY

Description	Amount

WEEKLY EXPENSE TRACKER

TOTAL EXPENSES		BALANCE	

FRIDAY

Description	Amount

SATURDAY

Description	Amount

SUNDAY

Description	Amount

NOTES

WEEKLY EXPENSES TRACKER

MONTH		BUDGET	

MONDAY

Description	Amount

TUESDAY

Description	Amount

WEDNESDAY

Description	Amount

THURSDAY

Description	Amount

WEEKLY EXPENSE TRACKER

TOTAL EXPENSES		BALANCE	

FRIDAY

Description	Amount

SATURDAY

Description	Amount

SUNDAY

Description	Amount

NOTES

CPSIA information can be obtained
at www.ICGtesting.com
Printed in the USA
BVHW010257311219
568234BV00012B/450/P

9 781084 179417